# HARRY STYLES

## ANNUAL 2013

### POSY EDWARDS

D1119983

HELLO HARRY

# HELLO HARRY

Green eyes. Tousled, curly brown hair. Devilishly handsome, and dashingly cute. We are of course talking about Harry Edward Styles, the leader of the biggest boyband sensation of the century – One Direction.

Harry has come a long way from his humble beginnings in the small, sleepy village of Holmes Chapel in Cheshire. Harry has sung his way from behind a karaoke machine to school plays, to a band he formed with friends – and finally, onto the stage of the *X Factor*.

Although Harry didn't make it through on his own, fate threw him together with Louis, Zayn, Liam and Niall. Together, the boys are One Direction – and they are unstoppable!

But what does Harry look for in a girlfriend? What was he good at in school? And what does he wear to bed?? Find out the answers to these questions, plus all the latest Harry and One Direction gossip and news inside!

**FUN FACT:**
Although he's a brunette now, Harry's hair was white-blonde when he was born – and the first word he ever said was 'cat'!

I ♥ HARRY

**FUN FACT:**
Harry's middle name
is Edward.

# Chapter 1
# MEET MR HARRY STYLES!

## ☆ Mr Harry Styles!

Harry Styles was born on 1st February 1994, in Cheshire to mum Anne and dad Des. The green-eyed, curly-haired cutey was always a performer, and was treading the boards in plays, acting and singing almost as soon as he could walk!

When he was younger, his favourite artist was Elvis. Harry and his dad used to listen to Elvis songs together, and Harry would sing along to the tunes on a karaoke machine.

## ☆ Tough times for the family

Harry remembers his early years being pretty great, playing endlessly with his older sister Gemma and their friends. But then, when he was just seven years old, his mum and dad got divorced.

'That was quite a weird time,' remembers Harry. 'I remember crying about it when my parents told me they were splitting up. I guess I didn't really get what was going on properly, I was just sad that my parents wouldn't be together anymore.'

## HARRY THE DRAMA KING

**Harry always loved performing on stage. He dressed up as a church mouse in a play called *Barney*, and wore his sister's grey tights and headband for the show! He once even dressed up as Buzz Lightyear from *Toy Story* in a performance of *Chitty Chitty Bang Bang* – pretty off the wall, but that's our Harry!**

After his parents split up, Harry and his sister moved away from their family home in the village of Holmes Chapel. They moved to a pub where his mum became the new landlady. But Harry stayed strong through the family upheaval, and managed to keep his head above water at school. In the hot summers, he would cycle to get ice cream from the Great Budworth Ice Cream Farm near his house – the exact same place he took the other members of One Direction when they stayed with him before the *X Factor* bootcamp!

## School Days

Harry always had a large group of friends and he did really well at English and sports at school. But being so creative, Harry preferred chatting to his mates to studying and found himself endlessly daydreaming. But when he made the move to secondary school, Harry vowed to try harder. He concentrated more in class, and started playing more sport.

## White Eskimo

When he was in Year Eight, Harry made friends with Will Sweeny, a drummer at his school who wanted to start a band with a couple of other school friends. They asked Harry to try out to be their singer, much to Harry's surprise!

Although he loved singing when he was a child, Harry hadn't really sung anywhere apart from in the shower. But he thought being in a band would be pretty awesome, so they started practising together. They rehearsed songs like 'Summer of 69' by Bryan Adams and 'Be My Girl' by Jet, getting ready for a local Battle of the Bands competition.

The band had a lot of fun rehearsing together, but they couldn't think of a name for themselves. 'It got to the day before the show and we had to put something down, so we decided to just go for something completely random,' says Harry. 'I suggested White Eskimo, and we hadn't thought of anything better … so that's who we were!'

The band made it through to the finals of the competition, and ended up winning!

## Family happiness

When Harry was 12, he and sister Gemma moved back to Holmes Chapel with their mum, and it was at this time that mum Anne met her new partner, Robin. Harry got on well with Robin, but mum Anne was nervous about spending too much time with him because she wanted to make sure Harry and Gemma were happy about the change. But luckily for Anne, Harry and Gemma liked Robin a lot, and Harry even used to text him to invite him over.

The kids were thrilled when Robin proposed to Anne, especially Harry, who had always been very close to his mum. 'I'm really close to my dad Des as well,' says Harry. 'He's very supportive of everything I'm doing. I think we're probably quite alike in lots of ways.'

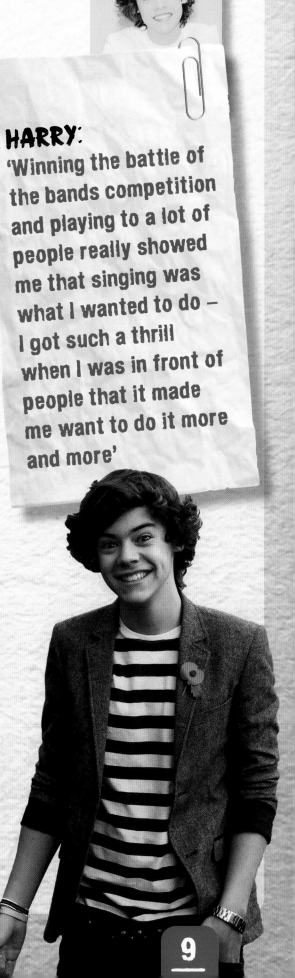

**HARRY:**
'Winning the battle of the bands competition and playing to a lot of people really showed me that singing was what I wanted to do – I got such a thrill when I was in front of people that it made me want to do it more and more'

## The road to *X Factor*

After their success in the Battle of the Bands competition, White Eskimo decided to take their career a little more seriously and started putting more energy into their rehearsals, meeting every Wednesday night after school to practise. Soon they were rewarded with their first gig – a girl at their school asked them to play at her mum's wedding, and so White Eskimo started rehearsing 25 songs that the bride had requested.

White Eskimo's first paid gig went really well for them; the crowd loved the songs, and after they'd played, one of the guests at the wedding (who was a music producer) approached the band and told them he thought they had real talent. Motivated and inspired by their reception at the wedding, White Eskimo spent more time in rehearsals and became serious about pursuing a career in music. Drummer Will's mum is TV presenter, Yvette Fielding, and she encouraged the band, giving them advice about how to make it in the pop music industry.

**HARRY:**

'I had always thought about going in for the *X Factor*, and watching Eoghan Quigg and Lloyd Daniels in 2009, who were young lads like me, made me want to do it even more.'

## Ambition

Inspired by White Eskimo's success, Harry decided that he would take the plunge and see if he had what it takes to make it on the *X Factor*. Faced with filling in the application form, Harry started to doubt his abilities and decided not to bother, convinced he wouldn't get through anyway.

But mum Anne was always there, backing him up – and she ended up filling in the application and sending it off for him! 'I often have those moments when I think, "What if she hadn't done that?"' Harry said later. 'If I hadn't gone in for the *X Factor*, I would have still been in college!'

I ❤ HARRY

**FUN FACT:**
Harry loves a nice cup of tea, and definitely prefers tea to coffee.

# Harry's favourites...

**FAVOURITE MOVIES:** *The Notebook, Titanic, Love Actually*

**FAVOURITE ALBUM:** *21* by Adele

**FAVOURITE TV SHOW:** *Family Guy*

**FAVOURITE SHOP:** Selfridges

**FAVOURITE COLOUR:** Orange

**FAVOURITE RESTAURANT:** TGI Fridays

**FAVOURITE LOVE SONG:** 'Lady In Red' by Chris de Burgh

**FAVOURITE BANDS:** The Beatles, Queen, Elvis, Coldplay

# HOT HARRY QUIZ

How much do you know about the hottest member of One Direction? Check your knowledge in our Hot Harry quiz!

1. **Which accents are Harry's favourites?**
   - Spanish and American
   - French and Australian
   - Norwegian and Japanese
   - German and Canadian

2. **If Harry could meet anyone, who would it be?**
   - Elvis
   - The Queen
   - Freddie Mercury
   - David Beckham

3. **What's the first thing Harry notices about a girl?**
   - Hair
   - Eyes
   - Clothes
   - Shoes

4. **If Harry could eat only one thing for the rest of his life, what would it be?**
   - Pizza
   - Pasta
   - Salad
   - Tacos

5. **What is Harry's pet peeve?**
   - Swearing
   - Being messy
   - Snoring
   - Not finishing everything on your plate

6. **What is Harry's favourite Starbucks drink?**
   - Skinny latte
   - Decaf cappuccino
   - Mango and passion fruit smoothie
   - Mocaccino

7. **What is Harry's favourite type of cake?**
   - Chocolate
   - Victoria sponge
   - Lemon drizzle
   - Carrot

8. **If Harry could have dinner with any three people from any period in time, who would he choose?**
   - Elvis Presley, Freddie Mercury and Michael Jackson
   - Lady Gaga, Madonna and Barack Obama
   - Cheryl Cole, Pixie Lott and Jimi Hendrix
   - Dale Winton, Dermot O'Leary and Noel Gallagher

9. **What is Harry's favourite ice cream flavour?**
   - Chocolate
   - Vanilla
   - Honeycomb
   - Rum and raisin

10. **How does Harry like his eggs?**
- **Boiled**
- **Scrambled**
- **Fertilised**
- **Raw**

11. **Harry always bites two Twix bars at the same time, because he doesn't want either of the sticks to feel lonely. True or false?**
- **True**
- **False**

12. **Harry loves when girls give him cutesie nicknames like 'snugglebug' and 'woogleybear'. True or false?**
- **True**
- **False**

13. **Harry sleeps without any clothes on. True or false?**
- **True**
- **False**

14. **One of Harry's friends once convinced him to eat Jaffa cakes with brown sauce on them. True or false?**
- **True**
- **False**

15. **What three things would Harry want if he was stranded on a desert island?**
- **His phone, phone charger and eletricity**
- **A football, his iPod and sweets**
- **His mum, dad and sister**

Answers on page 62

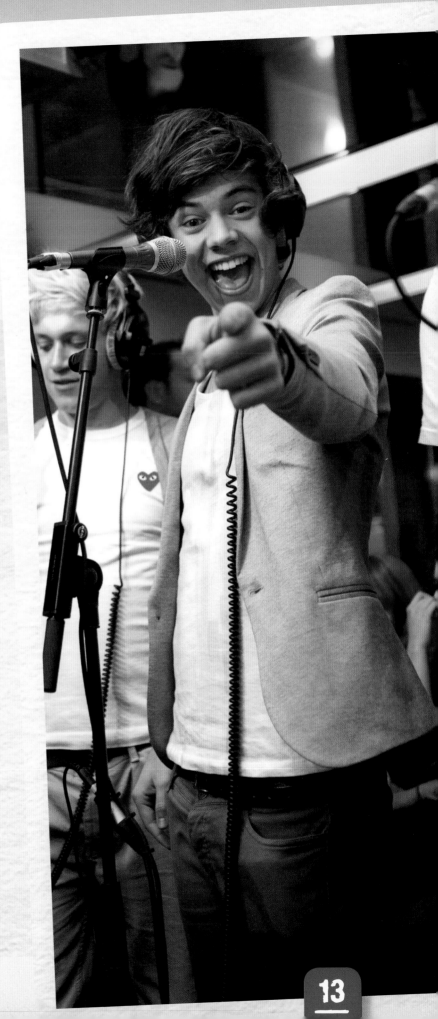

# Chapter 2

## THE X FACTOR ROLLERCOASTER

After making it through the initial audition stages, the boys lined up nervously to hear their fate and whether or not they had got through to the next round: the Judges' Houses. They were all destroyed when they heard that none of them had. 'I honestly thought that was the end of everything, I was so upset,' says Liam.

Lady Luck was smiling on them that day – or at least, Nicole Scherzinger was! Seeing that the five lads had a similar style and were around the same age, she suggested putting together them together as a group, to be tutored by Simon Cowell.

The boys were all speechless – to get a second chance like that was virtually unheard of in the competition. They didn't have to think twice about saying yes!

**I ♥ HARRY**

**FUN FACT:** As well as being vocally talented, Harry is very musical. He also plays the kazoo!

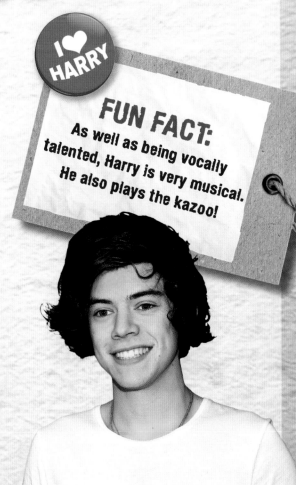

## Bonding at Harry's house ☆

As soon as the boys were put in the band, Harry immediately invited the boys up to his stepdad Robin's bungalow in Cheshire for a week of band practice and bonding. The boys all put in some money and Harry's mum put a load of food in the fridge for them, and then left them to get on with their work.

The time at the bungalow was an important bonding experience for the boys. They shared everything with each other, talking about their families and friends and also their hopes and dreams for the future.

'I think it is incredible how we'd met so recently and within a week we felt like best friends. It wasn't forced in any way, it just happened naturally,' says Louis. With any other group of five lads, things might have ended up being very different indeed.

It wasn't all serious stuff though. The boys also had a lot of fun in their week at the bungalow. There were blow-up mattresses everywhere, so people would just crash out wherever they were, day or night!

The boys spent the days in the swimming pool or watching TV. They tried to rehearse, but they didn't really know what they were doing! 'We'd sit around and sing what we thought were harmonies and try out different songs, but really that week was more about us getting used to each other than anything else,' says Niall.

## ☆ Judges' Houses: the trip to Spain

Spain was a learning curve for the boys, where they started to get on really well as a group. 'It was so, so weird,' says Harry. 'We were still getting to know each other and then all of a sudden we were getting on a plane together for what felt like a holiday.' They bonded even more, ate pizza together, and enjoyed some Spanish sunshine.

The boys put in more hours of serious practice, and their obvious bond with each other showed in their performances.

**LOUIS:**
'Harry and I bonded immediately and he's now my best mate in the band. He's such a cool guy and very laid-back and easy to talk to. I feel like I've known him for so much longer than I have. I guess we've got a bit of a bromance going on!'

I ♥ HARRY

**FUN FACT:** Harry is very ticklish.

They were rewarded with a place in the live finals! But on the plane on the way back to the UK, although they wanted to celebrate, the boys were careful – they didn't want to brag in front of all the other people who wouldn't be making it any further in the competition. 'I wanted to tell the world!' says Harry. 'I was so happy!'

## Rest and relaxation

When they returned from Spain, all the boys headed back to their respective homes for a couple of days of serious chilling. For Harry, this meant hitting the shops to get some cool clothes for the live shows.

Heading back to London, it was time for One Direction to move into the house where they'd be living with the rest of the contestants for the next few weeks. Sharing a room was a bit of a shock for the boys at that time, as the room they had together was pretty small, and there wasn't much chance for time on their own.

'It did get pretty grotty, because you can imagine what it's like with five teenage boys sharing such a small space!' says Harry.

**ZAYN:**
'I felt like I was having a spell in the army. You don't watch TV, you don't know what's going on in the outside world, and all that matters to you is the competition, so you can feel a bit detached from reality.'

**HARRY**
'I have so many great memories of being in the house.'

## ☆ *The X Factor*: The Big Final

On that fateful weekend in December, One Direction took their place alongside contestants Cher Lloyd, Matt Cardle, and Rebecca Ferguson. 'So excited!!!' tweeted Harry, in the afternoon before the Saturday show. The atmosphere backstage was super tense. All the boys knew that absolutely everything was riding on this. They had been so lucky to get this far in the competition, especially after they had all been initially disqualified!

The finalists had all been paired up with celebrity partners to perform duets on the show: Matt Cardle sang 'Unfaithful' with Bajan beauty Rihanna; Rebecca Ferguson sang 'Beautiful' with Christina Aguilera; Cher Lloyd sang 'Where Is The Love / I Got A Feeling' with will.i.am; and One Direction sang 'She's The One' with boyband veteran and pop legend, Robbie Williams. The audience screamed and screamed for One Direction. If the results had gone on volume alone, they definitely would have won!

The contestants all took to the stage to hear the result. One act would be eliminated that night, with three final acts going on to compete against each other on the Sunday show.

The boys all stood on stage, with their fingers crossed behind their backs. And Lady Luck was smiling again – as it was Cher Lloyd who was eliminated. One Direction had made it through!

I ♥ HARRY

**FUN FACT:**
Harry has been known to talk in his sleep.

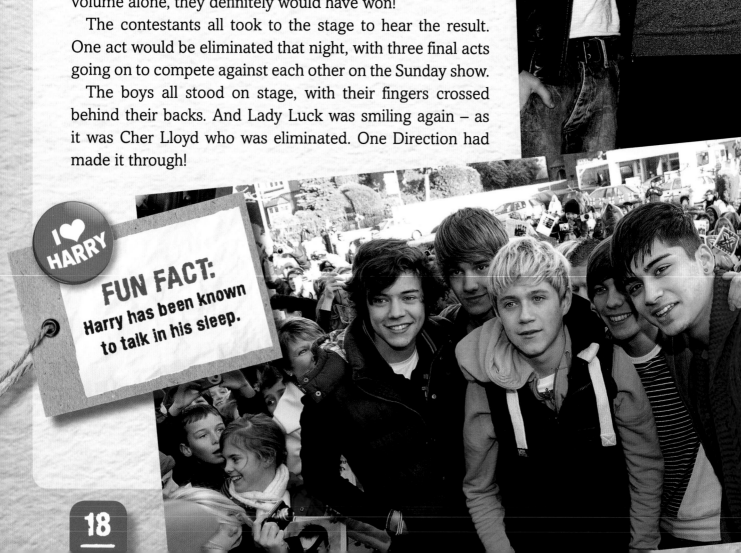

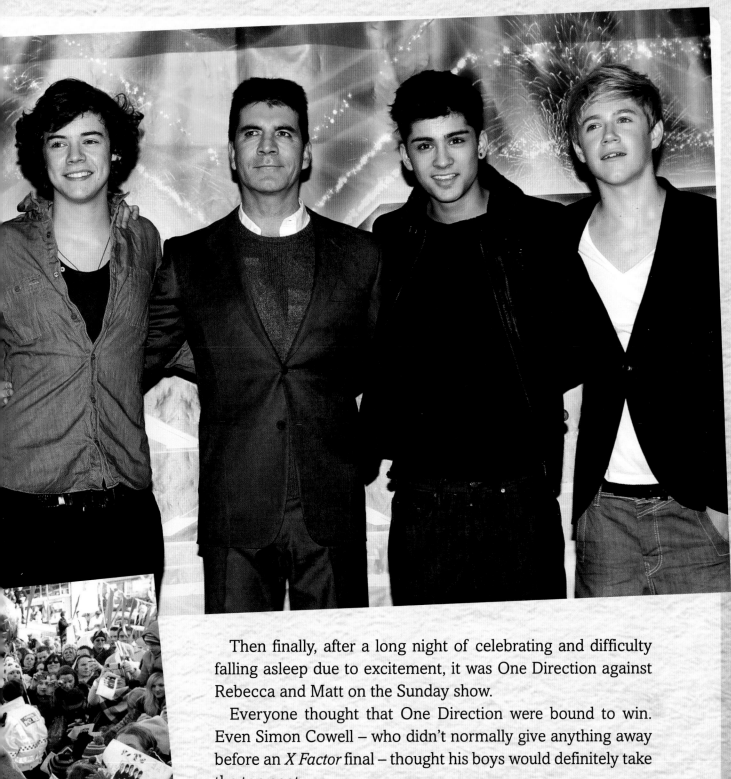

Then finally, after a long night of celebrating and difficulty falling asleep due to excitement, it was One Direction against Rebecca and Matt on the Sunday show.

Everyone thought that One Direction were bound to win. Even Simon Cowell – who didn't normally give anything away before an *X Factor* final – thought his boys would definitely take the top spot.

'I've got to know them well over the last few weeks and they have been so much fun to work with,' he said. 'They're just great. Have you seen the way they are with their fans? Even though it's freezing cold, they're out there the whole time, they talk to them, they respect them. They appreciate every single call that is being made, they are those kinds of guys.'

The boys gave a passionate performance of the song 'Torn', but after Rebecca's version of 'Sweet Dreams (Are Made Of This)' and Matt's 'Firework', it just wasn't enough. One Direction were eliminated.

'I'm absolutely gutted,' said Simon Cowell. 'But this is just the beginning for these boys.'

One Direction had come third, with Rebecca Ferguson coming in second, and Matt Cardle announced as the winner.

The boys walked off with their heads held high, but as soon as they came off stage, Harry, Zayn and Niall were in floods of tears.

But Louis and Liam were both more level-headed about the result. 'All the other boys were gutted, but I had a feeling that we'd be okay,' says Liam. I kept thinking about other people who hadn't won and had done well anyway. Diana Vickers came fourth – and look at where she is now.'

## A tense situation

After the enormous disappointment of the final, the boys pulled themselves together emotionally and then decided that, no matter what, they would still try to make it. They had come so far and worked so hard, and they were a far cry from the rag-tag group of teenagers who had been thrown together as a group just weeks earlier.

Then they received the call – Simon Cowell wanted to see them in his dressing room!

Never one to give away good news straight away, Simon made the boys play the waiting game while he told them how much he liked them as a group. They stood there, terrified, waiting for him to give them a definite answer – and then he told them he wanted to sign them. Filled with emotion, Harry cried with joy this time! 'I sat there thinking, why am I crying? If this works out it's going to totally change my life!' he says. Harry couldn't have known how right he was…

## One Direction: the group together

One Direction were officially a pop group, and signed with Syco Records in a massive two million pound deal. But Simon Cowell wasn't giving them a licence to relax – in fact, he told the boys he was giving them a music industry lifeline and he expected a lot from them in return.

The boys swore they would work incredibly hard and give everything they had to make One Direction a success.

But there was little time for celebration. The very next morning, One Direction moved out of the contestants' house and into a swanky hotel in West London where they spent a whirlwind week of management meetings, contract discussions, and promotional shows where the boys flexed their vocal muscle and showed off what they could do.

They went on to play countless shows and perform on TV, and before they knew it, Christmas had rolled around, giving them all some time to relax from the craziness of the *X Factor* rollercoaster!

**I ♥ HARRY**

**FUN FACT:** Cheeky Harry once shaved a letter H into Zayn's leg hair while Zayn was asleep!

**LIAM:** 'The number of girls wearing 'I Love Harry' t-shirts is unbelievable. They love him!'

I ♥ HARRY

**FUN FACT:**
Harry is scared of snakes.

## A quick festive break ☆

'I think we were all looking forward to having a break over Christmas,' says Harry. 'I missed the boys quite a lot, but at the same time it was great to just relax and see my family. Loads of my friends wanted to catch up so things were quite busy, but I didn't want people to think that I'd changed and I didn't have time for them.'

All the boys needed the break and to have time to reconnect with their families and friends back home, and also time to make up for all that lost sleep!

Harry also made time for some Twitter fun by taking part in live stream chats with fans. 'Loved the Twitcam Rampage....,' he tweeted, after having been online all day. 'Have a good day everyone :D x' He also asked fans to tweet him some questions under the #askharry hashtag, giving his supporters some attention!

He was asked what his best memory of being on *X Factor* was, to which he replied 'getting to the final with the boys :)'. He was also asked what his favourite song was, which, at the time, was 'Grenade' by Bruno Mars. And one fan asked what was next for the One Direction boys… to which he replied 'you'll have to wait and see :)'.

## The gang back together

As soon as the Christmas break was over, the boys were back to work. They warmed up by playing some shows and a few private industry parties – and then they were hit with amazing news – they were off to the sunshine of LA to do some recording! Word of the One Direction party had already spread to America, where a crowd of screaming fans were waiting at the airport for the boys, with huge banners declaring their love!

The boys met megastars like Randy Jackson and Bryan McFadden, and got to record with RedOne, a producer who collaborates with Lady Gaga. They stayed in the W hotel, a famous celeb hangout, and made the most of the weather by getting up early every morning and hanging out in the hotel's pool.

Although they were there to work, they had no set schedule, and so quite often the boys found themselves at a loose end. But they made the most of their leisure time, and hit the shops! 'I literally raided Abercrombie and Fitch,' confides Harry. 'Louis reckons I bought every single T-shirt in there. I think he's exaggerating, but I did get quite a few…' In fact, the boys were so enjoying the retail therapy that Zayn and Liam almost missed the plane!

Landing back in the UK, the boys had their first taste of proper stardom when they were mobbed at Heathrow airport. There wasn't much security, and so there was no one to shield the boys from the hundreds of screaming fans stampeding towards them. Liam accidentally got hit in the face in the scuffle to escape, and Harry and Louis had clothes ripped off them as they ran for safety!

## ☆ The *X Factor* Live tour

As soon as they were back from America, One Direction were taken to rehearsals for the *X Factor Live* tour. The boys wanted to put on an amazing show, and worked really hard to pick up new dance routines and learn how to interact more with the crowd.

**FUN FACT:** Harry has many secret talents – one of which is knowing how to knit.

It was tough, especially learning dance moves when none of the boys had ever been trained as dancers before.

But it was all worth it when they hit the stage for the tour's first night, in Liam's hometown of Birmingham. Crowds of screaming girls welcomed them onto the stage, and then screamed extra loud nearly all the way through the boys' performance.

'Getting to put everything we'd learnt into practise on tour was the ultimate pay-off for all the hard work we'd done,' says Harry.

## Boys will be boys

Although the boys were working hard, rehearsing and practising their dancing and their harmonies, they still found time to play pranks. One night, Louis started throwing fruit at his bandmates, and before they knew it, they were all throwing fruit at each other, making a complete mess of the backstage area! They did get a bit of a telling off for that. But boys will be boys!

Although the tour was hard work – playing over 60 gruelling shows – the boys loved getting to hang out with everyone from the TV series. And Harry loved the tour so much he didn't feel homesick at all, although he felt guilty about that later. But he never wanted the tour to end!

Eventually, when the *X Factor Live* tour was finally over, the boys had the opportunity to get home, see their families, and have some well-deserved rest and relaxation. But not everyone was that keen to get home. 'End of the tour,' Harry posted on his Twitter. 'It's been the best time of my life, thank you for everything. And thanks to the boys.. you guys are like family..love you .x'

To get a little downtime in before they started work again, Harry, Louis and some friends went skiing in France. 'I had the best time ever,' he said. 'We had such a laugh!'

# ONE DIRECTION CUPCAKE PARTY!

Invite some friends round, get *Up All Night* on your iPod, cue up the music videos and have a One Direction cupcake party! These cupcakes are super easy to make and super tasty… you can even add food colouring to the batter to make the cakes whatever colour you like! Always remember to get an adult to help you in the kitchen.

### Step 1
Turn on the oven and preheat it to 170°C/325°F/gas mark 3.

### Step 2
Line a 12-hole cupcake tin with paper cases.

### Step 3
In the food processor, mix together the butter, sugar, eggs and vanilla until smooth. Also add the food colouring here if you want to use it. If you have a favourite member of 1D, you could make the batter their favourite colour! Remember that Harry's favourite colour is orange, Zayn and Louis's favourite colour is red, Niall's favourite colour is blue and Liam's favourite colour is purple!

### Step 4
Once those are all mixed, add the flour and mix that in.

### Step 5
Spoon the mixture into your paper cases.

### Step 6
Bake for 15-20 minutes until golden and springy to the touch.

### Step 7
Add the icing to the tops, and then you can decorate each one with a funky 1D logo! Feel free to add sprinkles, sherbet, or anything else you like!

## Makes 12 cupcakes

### Ingredients

4oz/115g butter, at room temperature
4oz/115g caster sugar
2 large eggs, at room temperature
half a teaspoon vanilla extract
1-2 drops food colouring (if you want)
4oz/115g self-raising flour
sugar icing for the tops

# WORDSEARCH

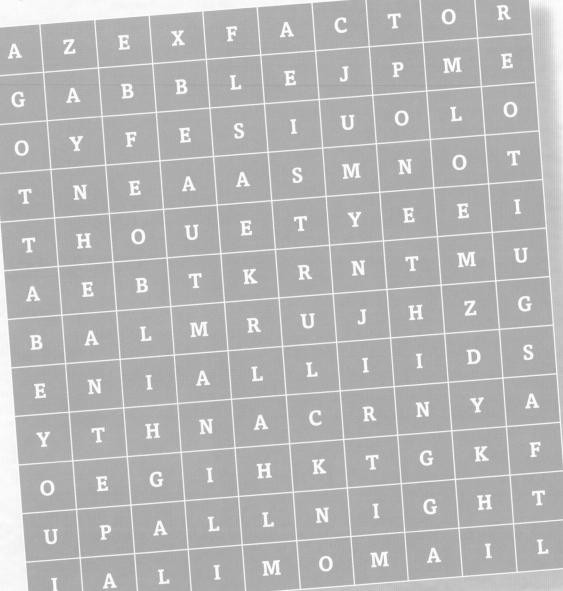

| A | Z | E | X | F | A | C | T | O | R |
| G | A | B | B | L | E | J | P | M | E |
| O | Y | F | E | S | I | U | O | L | O |
| T | N | E | A | A | S | M | N | O | T |
| T | H | O | U | E | T | Y | E | E | I |
| A | E | B | T | K | R | N | T | M | U |
| B | A | L | M | R | U | J | H | Z | G |
| E | N | I | A | L | L | I | I | D | S |
| Y | T | H | N | A | C | R | N | Y | A |
| O | E | G | I | H | K | T | G | K | F |
| U | P | A | L | L | N | I | G | H | T |
| I | A | L | I | M | O | M | A | I | L |

Harry          Louis          Gotta be You
Liam           Zayn           One Thing
Niall          Up All Night   X Factor

## Across

1. What is Harry's favourite colour?
2. Who gave the boys their multi-million pound record deal?
3. Where did the One Direction boys record their first song?
4. Who did One Direction support on tour in the US?
5. What is Harry's middle name?

## Down

1. What position did the One Direction song 'What Makes You Makes Beautiful' reach in the charts?
2. What is Harry's favourite shop in London?
3. Who is Harry's best friend in the band?
4. Where did the One Direction boys win 'Best British Single 2012'?
5. Who was Harry's favourite music artist growing up?

Answers on page 62

# Chapter 3
## ONE DIRECTION MEET THE BOYS!

# LOUIS TOMLINSON

Even from a young age, Louis was always really outgoing. He would chatter away to anyone who would come close enough to lend an ear and listen! He spent his childhood in Poole near Bournemouth, and then moved to Doncaster. He was a loud and confident kid, and often called the class clown by everyone who knew him.

Louis is the oldest of five children – he has younger sisters Lottie, Fizzy, and twins Daisy and Phoebe. He loves being part of a big family, although he and his father always had to stick together as the only men in a house with five women in it!

## Musical beginnings

When Louis was 14, he joined a band called The Rogue. He was on a school trip with some friends, who told him they were looking for a singer for their band, and asked if he would be interested in singing for them – even though they had never heard him sing! They played a lot of rock, especially songs by Green Day, and practised together once a week.

The band performed for the school year at the end of every term. After a year and a half, the band split up, but Louis and bandmate Stan kept the band's name and started working with another friend called Ben. They played some acoustic shows, but Louis never thought they would make it big: 'I just loved the feeling of performing to an audience,' he says.

**HARRY:**
'As a band, we're having the absolute best time ever. We've become better friends than I ever could have imagined and it's so nice to have four other lads to share this experience with.'

## Treading the boards

The love of performing had also led Louis to acting in school shows, including landing the lead role of Danny in a school performance of *Grease*. Louis also appeared as an extra on the TV show *Fat Friends*, which was where he first met the actor James Corden, who is now good friends with all of One Direction. How times change!

Louis went on to play small parts in other TV dramas, but he passed the days doing odd jobs between acting roles, like waiting tables, working the tills at football club Doncaster Rovers, and working at the local cinema, which he really loved as he got to see all the new films for free.

**LOUIS FUN FACT:**

Harry and Louis bonded immediately, says Harry: 'I got on with Louis from the word go. We're very similar and I like the fact that he has this ability to be nice to everyone while living totally for the moment. It puts a smile on your face when you see someone like that. I feel I can tell him anything, and I felt like that straight away. He can be really funny one minute, but if someone has a problem he can go into serious mode straight away and he gives really good advice.'

## A step backwards

It was a real blow to Louis when he failed his first year of A-levels. He was gutted, as his school wouldn't let him re-sit. 'All of my good friends had passed, and I knew they would be going back the next year and then heading off to university and I'd be left behind.' Although he had to join another school, outgoing Louis soon managed to make new friends and worked hard.

Louis had entered the *X Factor* once before, in 2009, and been rejected – he hadn't even made it past the first round. So second time around, he was more determined and driven than he had ever been in his whole life.

**What Louis looks for in a girl:**

'I don't have a specific look, but I like a girl who is spontaneous and bubbly and has a good sense of humour. And someone chatty like me. I do like being in relationships. I wasn't one to play the field when I was younger, and I can't imagine being like that now.'

# Louis factfile

**BIRTHDAY:** 24th December 1991

**STAR SIGN:** Capricorn

**FAVOURITE FILMS:** *Grease*

**FAVOURITE ALBUM:** *21* by Adele, *How To Save A Life* by The Fray

**FAVOURITE TV SHOWS:** *Skins, One Tree Hill*

**FAVOURITE FOOD:** Pizza, pasta

**FAVOURITE COLOUR:** Red

# ZAYN MALIK

Zayn has always loved big families, and has five aunties and two uncles just on his dad's side. The only boy in a family with three sisters, Zayn was brought up around girls and is very respectful of women. 'I also think I understand women more than the average man does, to be honest!' he laughs.

He was always a handful as a child, because he had so much energy. He was really sensitive to sugar, so even the smallest amount of it would mean he was bouncing off the walls.

**ZAYN:**
'As much as I love meeting people, I like to get to know people properly before I think of them as real friends.'

## Star in the making

Zayn's granddad was born in Pakistan and his dad was born in England, and Zayn's mum had one English parent and one Irish parent. 'So I'm Irish/English/Asian, which is quite a mix!' he says.

His confidence led to auditioning for some school plays, including small parts in *Arabian Nights* and *Grease,* and the lead part of Bugsy in *Bugsy Malone*. At that time, though he enjoyed singing, it was all about acting for Zayn – he loved the feeling of being on stage, playing a character. In the end, it was his music teacher that suggested he try out for the *X Factor*.

## Towards the big time... ☆

He got the application form when he was 15, but he decided that he wasn't ready to try out. He did the same thing again when he was 16, but then when he was 17, he was finally ready to send it off. Even then, when it came to the audition, Zayn hid in bed and refused to get up. In the end it was his mother who had to order him up and out of the house!

'I was scared of being rejected, so when I kept getting through to the next stage it was just crazy,' he says. 'I thought they were only putting me through for a joke and that people were laughing at how bad I was.'

But Zayn ended up making it through to the final and beyond, in One Direction. 'It feels so strange when I look back to before the *X Factor*, when I didn't even have a passport and had never even been to London, never mind outside the UK. Now all of a sudden I've been to all these amazing places!'

**ZAYN FUN FACT:**
When he was 13, Zayn started paying serious attention to his looks. He even used to get up half an hour earlier than his sisters so he could do his hair!

# Zayn factfile

**BIRTHDAY:** 12th December 1993

**STAR SIGN:** Capricorn

**FAVOURITE FILMS:** *Freedom Writers*

**FAVOURITE ALBUM:** *Where I Wanna Be* by Donnell Jones

**FAVOURITE TV SHOWS:** *Family Guy*

**FAVOURITE FOOD:** Nandos

**FAVOURITE COLOUR:** Red

# NIALL HORAN

Baby faced cutie Niall grew up in the small town of Mullingar in the midlands of Ireland. His parents split up when he was five, and after spending a few years living between his mum's house and his dad's house, Niall finally ended up moving in with his dad, who lived in town, which was easier for Niall to see his friends and get to school.

He only has one sibling – older brother Greg – and they never got along when Niall was growing up. 'We hated each other!' says Niall. But now the brothers have grown up, they love each other and get along great.

He was always small for his age, but luckily he was never bullied at school as he always tried to be friendly with everyone. He was very musical and was always singing one thing or another as a child.

'Once we were driving along, I was singing Garth Brooks in the back of the car and my aunt said she thought the radio was on!' remembers Niall. He first picked up a guitar at the age of 12, and entered a few local competitions singing and playing guitar, and became well known in his small town for being a local music talent.

**NIALL:** 'It's what we've always dreamed of doing.'

## Head in the clouds

He managed to do okay through school, but Niall was always dreaming of other things, or messing around playing football with his mates. 'I thought school was all about having a crack and acting like a fool,' he says. He found subjects like Maths hard, but was good at languages, picking up French and Spanish very quickly.

The Spanish came in handy for when he was in Marbella being coached by Simon Cowell, as Niall could then translate things for the other One Direction boys!

He always loved pop music, and his musical heroes were Irish band Westlife. His other favourite bands are The Script, The Coronas, The Eagles, Thin Lizzy, and Take That!

Niall always wanted a future in music. In fact, his plans were to go to university and study sound engineering, but those plans were put on hold when he made it through to the live rounds of the *X Factor*.

## Niall factfile

**BIRTHDAY:** 13th September 1993

**STAR SIGN:** Virgo

**FAVOURITE FILMS:** *Grease*, *Goodfellas*, the *Godfather* films

**FAVOURITE ALBUM:** *Crazy Love* by Michael Bublé

**FAVOURITE TV SHOWS:** *Two and a Half Men*

**FAVOURITE FOOD:** Nandos, pizza

**FAVOURITE COLOUR:** Blue

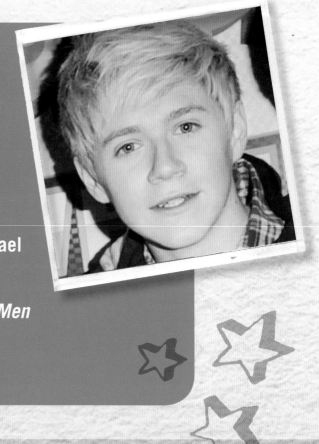

**What Niall looks for in a girl:**

'I like someone who can take a bit of banter, have a laugh, and likes the same things as me – if you go out with me you have to want to come to a football match. I support Derby County and I always have! I like a natural look on a girl.'

# LIAM PAYNE

**Liam has often been called the dad of the group because he always looks out for the rest of the guys and makes sure everyone is ok.**

He's also the clumsiest member of the group, and often ends up spilling drinks on himself or falling over things. He even went through a phase of accidentally ripping his trousers while performing onstage – a bit embarrassing, but all the screaming girls in the audience didn't mind!

## A difficult start

When he was born three weeks early the doctors flew into panic, as he had been born without a heartbeat. Though they managed to bring him round, his first few years were touch and go. Up to the age of four he was always falling ill.

Poor Liam had to go through hundreds of tests to try and work out what was wrong, and in the end they found out it was because he had one kidney that didn't work. Although Liam still has both of his kidneys, one of them doesn't function properly, so he has to be very careful with what he drinks to make sure he stays healthy.

## Determination

Despite his difficult start, Liam didn't let that stop him – he joined the Wolverhampton and Bilston running team, and was the third best over 1,500 metres for three years in a row!

**LIAM:**
'Working out is really important to me because it also takes out any stress.'

He also got into basketball at school, but ended up getting bullied at practice. Liam went to boxing lessons with his sister's boyfriend, and soon toughened up and learned how to defend himself. He was nearly kicked out of school for standing up to the bullies and fighting them (luckily, he won!).

## Finding his voice

In Year Nine at school, Liam joined the choir. Liam always loved singing, and used to sing karaoke all the time as a child. When he was 14, he first tried out for the *X Factor*. He had been training as a runner and was on the reserve list for the 2012 Olympics, but he was searching for something else he could do apart from running. So he decided to pursue singing more seriously.

**LIAM:** 'I had a photo taken with Harry at Bootcamp because I knew he was going to be famous.'

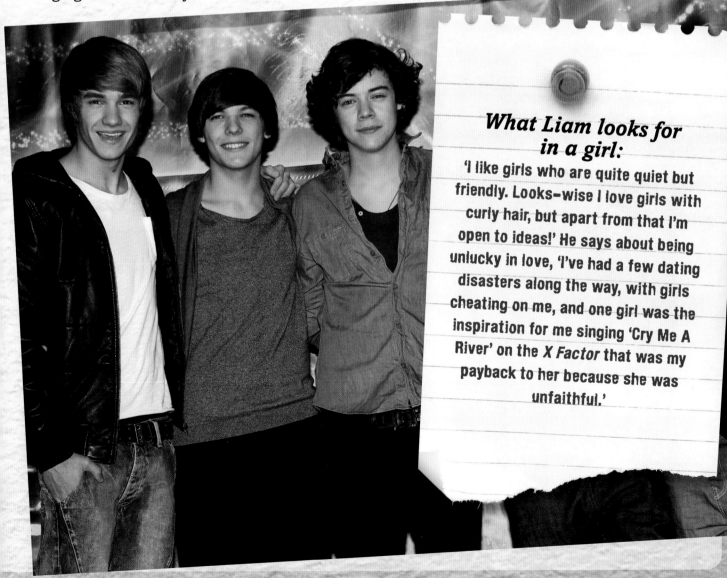

*What Liam looks for in a girl:*
'I like girls who are quite quiet but friendly. Looks-wise I love girls with curly hair, but apart from that I'm open to ideas!' He says about being unlucky in love, 'I've had a few dating disasters along the way, with girls cheating on me, and one girl was the inspiration for me singing 'Cry Me A River' on the *X Factor* that was my payback to her because she was unfaithful.'

## LIAM FUN FACT:

Liam was never very fashion conscious when he was younger, so when it came time for him to audition for the *X Factor*, he had nothing to wear! He borrowed a pair of Armani jeans, wore a large shirt and a waistcoat, and performed through the first three rounds of the show with a hole in his shoe. How things have changed now!

Unfortunately for Liam, though he felt like he was mature enough to handle the show, he was turned away at the Judge's House. Really though, that rejection was a blessing in disguise. 'Looking back now at all we've been through, there is no way I could have handled it,' said Liam wisely later. 'No way at all.'

Depressed after his taste of stardom after he was rejected, Liam went back to school, but he was distracted and his grades started slipping. But after a sharp talking to from his Head of Year, Liam pulled his socks up and started working really hard at school, getting great grades for his GCSEs. But Liam had been bitten by the music bug, and headed off to Music College. He practised his singing and made sure to perform live as much as he could, and then at the age of 16 decided it was time to give the *X Factor* another try.

# Liam factfile

**BIRTHDAY:** 29th August 1993

**STAR SIGN:** Virgo

**FAVOURITE FILMS:** *Click*, all the *Toy Story* films

**FAVOURITE ALBUM:** *Echo* by Leona Lewis

**FAVOURITE TV SHOWS:** *Friends*, *Everybody Loves Raymond*

**FAVOURITE FOOD:** Chocolate

**FAVOURITE COLOUR:** Purple

# ONE DIRECTION QUIZ

How well do you think you know Harry, Louis, Zayn, Liam and Niall
Test your One Direction knowledge now and find out!

1. Which member of One Direction would have had a future in a factory building planes or working as a fireman if he hadn't made it through the *X Factor*?

2. Whose first pet was a terrapin called Frederick?

3. Which member of One Direction gets the mickey taken out of him for being broody and wanting kids?

4. Which member of One Direction mentioned that he'd like some Curiously Cinnamon cereal on Twitter – only to find that a fan had brought some to the hotel they were staying in?

5. Which member of One Directions's mum recently revealed on Twitter the following fact about their son: 'When ___ was a toddler he used to sit in his buggy waving to everyone saying "Hiya, have a good day!"'

6. Whose celebrity crush is Megan Fox?

7. Which member of One Direction is scared of heights, scared of people messing about on stairs, scared of amusement rides and scared of the dark?

8. Which member of One Direction says their all time hero is Michael Bublé?

9. Which member of One Direction said 'I would like to carry on what we're doing and get bigger, better and stronger!'

10. Whose favourite drink is apple juice?

11. Which member of One Direction said 'I get on stage and I feel amazing. I'm so hyped up when I come off stage that I shout a lot and jump around! There's no feeling like it.'

12. Which member of One Direction makes a blink-and-you'll-miss-it appearance in Ed Sheeran's video for the song 'Drunk'?

Answers on page 62

# MAKE YOUR OWN 'I ♥ HARRY' T-SHIRT!

Do you want the world to know that you are 100% Team Harry? Why not design your own 'I Heart Harry' T-shirt? It's bound to turn heads and you'll stand out in any crowd! Remember to ask a grown-up for the needle and thread if you aren't very good at sewing!

## You will need:

**A plain T-shirt (preferably white, but any light colour will do)**

**Some newspaper**

**Fabric marker pens**

**Some red felt material (a little smaller than the front of your T-shirt)**

**A needle and thread**

**Fabric glitter glue**

## What to do:

Find a flat surface, like a dining room table. Lay your T-shirt flat on the table and place some newspaper over it. Now you need to draw a heart on the newspaper that will be the template for the red felt material for you to sew on your T-shirt. Make sure you draw the heart small enough so it fits on the T-shirt, but big enough that people will see it!

Then cut out the newspaper heart and use it as a template to cut out a red felt heart.

Place the red felt heart on the T-shirt where you want it to go, and then sew it into place. Remember to ask for help with the sewing if you need it. If someone at home has a sewing machine, you could ask them (very nicely!) to sew the heart on with the sewing machine for you.

Once the heart has been sewn on, then it's time to decorate! Use your markers to write 'I' above the heart and 'Harry' underneath – or you can be creative with where you place the words.

After you've written your essential message, get glittering with the fabric glitter glue! Draw swirls and whirls on the heart, or decorate the arms and back of your tee with some 1D logos and small glittery hearts.

Leave the glitter glue to dry (you may need to hang the T-shirt on a hanger for 24 hours, depending on the glue instructions).

If the marker pens and glue need to be ironed to be fixed in place, ask an adult to help you iron the designs.

And voila! Your very own I Heart Harry tee! Wear it with pride!

# Chapter 4
## STAYING UP ALL NIGHT!

After they had recovered from the X Factor Live tour, the boys worked super hard on their debut album because they wanted it to be perfect. They worked with their coach from the X Factor, Savan Kotecha, as well as producers Steve Robson and singer/songwriter Kelly Clarkson!

### Up All Night: recording the album

During the recording, the boys had a trip to Sweden and another trip to LA, where they stayed for three weeks, but unlike their last trip, this one was focused totally on finishing the album.

They had been writing songs throughout the *X Factor Live* tour, so when it came to having time in the studio, they were eager to put their own mark on the songs that had been written for them. The boys also wanted to recreate the boy band sound with their album, as there weren't many successful boy bands around anymore. 'We didn't want to be sitting on stools and singing ballads. We wanted some big songs that would surprise people,' says Niall.

The boys spent the summer of 2011 working on their debut album, and then finally, as the autumn drew near, the boys announced the lead single from the album – 'What Makes You Beautiful'.

I ♥ HARRY

**FUN FACT:**
Harry hates swearing, and gets annoyed if he hears the other boys cursing

**LIAM:**
'We don't have many days off, but we don't mind. We all push each other and support each other.'

**FUN FACT:**
Harry's favourite thing to have on toast is Nutella.

## ☆ 'What Makes You Beautiful'

'When we were recording in the studio we knew instantly that we wanted this track to be our first single,' says Harry. 'I think for us we wanted to release something that wasn't cheesy but it was fun. It kind of represented us, I think it took us a while to find it but I think we found the right song.'

That right song definitely was 'What Makes You Beautiful', written by Rami Yacoub, Carl Falk and the *X Factor* vocal coach Savan Kotecha, who, between them, had worked with the Backstreet Boys, Robyn, NSYNC, Taio Cruz, Nicole Scherzinger, and Matthew Morrison from Glee. Quite a hit list!

## One Direction are number one!

The single was released as a digital download on 11th September 2011, and smashed into the top spot in the UK Scottish and Irish singles charts, and came into the top ten in Australia, Belgium, Canada, and New Zealand. It even sold 100,000 copies after being available for only three days! The song has since sold nearly a million copies worldwide, and counting.

The music video for 'What Makes You Beautiful' was filmed in Malibu in California, and featured the five members of One Direction frolicking on the beach, driving up and down the coast in an orange campervan, and sitting around a campfire. The video, which was directed by John Urbano, had girls around the world swooning in unison, in particular at the part where Harry intimately serenaded a girl! Sigh…

## 'Gotta Be You' ☆

The second single from *Up All Night* is the big-sounding epic pop record, 'Gotta Be You'. The song was written for the boys by August Rigo (who has also written songs for Justin Bieber, Cheryl Cole and JLS) and veteran Steve Mac (who has written for The Saturdays, The Wanted, JLS, Ronan Keating, and Westlife). It was released on 11th November 2011, and made the top ten in the UK and Irish charts.

Though it didn't do quite as well as their first single, the song was still a hit – and it was helped along by having a video that was shot in Lake Placid in New York. It featured the boys wandering around some woods, hanging out by another campfire, and relaxing in a log cabin by a lake as the sun went down. Beautiful!

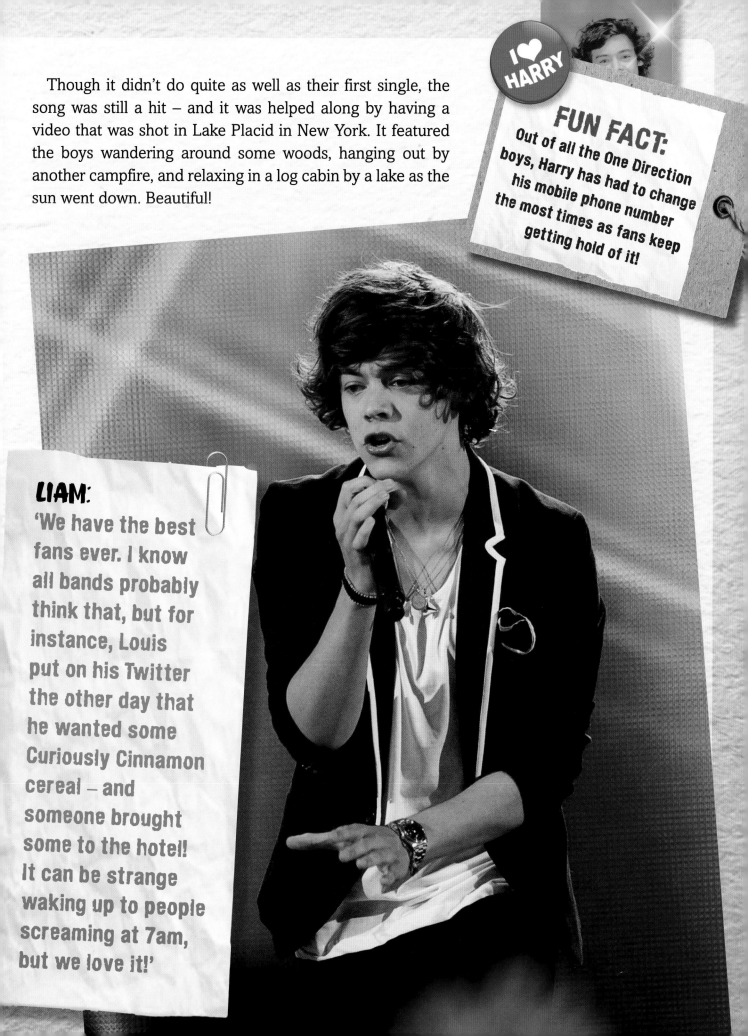

I ♥ HARRY

**FUN FACT:**
Out of all the One Direction boys, Harry has had to change his mobile phone number the most times as fans keep getting hold of it!

**LIAM:**
'We have the best fans ever. I know all bands probably think that, but for instance, Louis put on his Twitter the other day that he wanted some Curiously Cinnamon cereal – and someone brought some to the hotel! It can be strange waking up to people screaming at 7am, but we love it!'

**FUN FACT:**
Harry would love for his first child to be a baby girl, and he wants to name her Darcy.

## Pranks on set ☆

Although it was nice for the boys to get away to the quiet of the lake while they were shooting the video, they still had time to get in trouble – they all got a severe telling off for 'borrowing' a boat (without asking anyone!). They rowed it into the lake but then Louis and Liam started wrestling with each other, and Louis threw Liam into the water! Then they all started wrestling with each other and the boat capsized. The boys had to swim back to the shore, where they were given a tongue-lashing by a local security patrol!

And that wasn't the end of the fun. While they were filming, Zayn also accidentally crashed a scooter into a wall, and Louis broke the engine of the Mini he was driving. Oops!

## ☆ 'One Thing'

The third single from the album was the catchy, pop anthem 'One Thing', which had a particularly swoon-worthy video, showing the boys performing in and around London, including places like the steps at Trafalgar Square, Hampstead Heath park and on the top of a sightseeing bus driving around the sights of the city.

The song was released on 6th January 2012, and hit the top ten in the UK, Ireland, Australia, Hungary and Scotland. The song went into the American charts at number 35, but then two weeks later, when the video was released, the song jumped straight to number 10!

Not only did sales of the song go up after the video came out, but the number of fans they had on Facebook doubled, and the views of their videos on YouTube tripled! We always said these boys were easy on the eyes!

Despite his busy schedule, Harry still had time to squeeze in some more #askharry sessions on Twitter. He gave out his recommended cure for a lost voice ('don't talk, boiling water in a bowl and put a towel over your head and inhale the steam..drink lemon, honey and ginger!'), as well as that he had been listening to a lot of Coldplay on his iPod.

**NIALL:**
'I didn't realise how many fans we had until we went on tour.'

## ☆ The Brit Awards!

As if they hadn't already achieved enough, the boys then learnt they were up for a Brit Award for Best Single for 'What Makes You Beautiful'. 'I cannot believe we are up for a BRIT!!' tweeted Harry, when he found out. 'It's incredible what you guys have done for us… thank you so much. We love you!!'

Although they were nominated alongside more established artists like Jessie J, Olly Murs and The Wanted, there was no doubt who the public wanted to win – they wanted One Direction!

I ♥ HARRY

**FUN FACT:**
Harry loves going starkers. He's even been naked while riding a motorcycle!

'We cannot believe that we are stood here on this stage!' said Louis, accepting the award from Tinie Tempah. 'This award is for the fans. We would be absolutely nowhere without them, so thank you very much!'

The boys bounced off the stage and got into a group hug. Then Harry pulled his phone out to text everyone he knew back home, and to update his Twitter for all the One Direction fans. 'That was for all of you!' he tweeted. 'Thank you so much. You're amazing. Now.... Wooooooooooo!!!!!!!!!!!!'

**FUN FACT:**
Harry loves tasting food from other people's plates.

## ☆ The *Up All Night* tour

The tour supporting the *Up All Night* album was announced in September 2011, and tickets for the tour sold out within minutes of being on release. The boys hit the road, playing shows across Great Britain to thousands of screaming fans.

They then hopped over the water to America, to support the band Big Time Rush on their sold-out *Better With U* tour. Unfortunately, when they got there, Zayn had some bad news about the passing of a family member, and he had to fly back home for the funeral. Within a couple of days, he was back with the boys for when they started their UK and Ireland arena shows. 'Like he never left…!' tweeted Harry, posting a photo of Zayn in his sunnies, sticking his tongue out.

While they were in America, the boys did a whole bunch of signings, as they love the chance to meet up with fans. They also did some more promotion, including an appearance on *The Today Show*, where they almost couldn't get into the studio for the thousands of screaming girls outside desperate to catch a glance of their favourite boyband!

After more shows back in the UK, One Direction then flew over to Australia and New Zealand for more sold-out shows! What busy boys!

## Harry in the real world ⭐

After moving out of the *X Factor* bubble, Louis and Harry moved into a London flat together. It made sense for the boys, who've shared a 'bromance' since they met, to live together in a fun boy pad! Each of the other One Direction members was given their own swanky London flat, apart from Harry and Louis who shared a place. The boys were especially proud of their cinema room and their gym. Very nice!

## ☆ Growing up

But at the start of 2012, Harry finally felt it was time to spread his wings and get his own place. Flash with a bit of cash, Harry decided to invest in an east London pad for half a million pounds!

When Harry moved into his own place, many people wondered whether there were rifts growing between the One Direction boys. Harry had been seen on nights on the town away from his bandmates, with celebrity mates like DJ Nick Grimshaw. Was this the end of the team spirit that was the core of One Direction for so long?

Absolutely not! Although lots of people had focused on Harry as the leader of One Direction, he still thought of himself as part of the unit, and the stories about his new inflated ego really upset Harry. He had always prided himself on keeping his feet on the ground, and he was determined to stay that way.

## ON THE ROAD

Of all the things they do as a band, touring is definitely Harry's favourite. 'I love getting out on the road. We can see a lot more of the fans and they can see us performing our songs. It's down to us to show what we're all about, and we're looking forward to doing exactly that!'

I ♥ HARRY

**FUN FACT:**
When Harry was ten, he was attacked by a goat.

# MAKE YOUR OWN HARRY PICTURE FRAME!

Everyone has their own favourite photo of Harry... so why not put it in a dedicated, super-special customised frame? It's really easy to make a plain frame look great. Here's how!

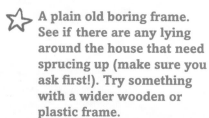

## You will need:

⭐ A plain old boring frame. See if there are any lying around the house that need sprucing up (make sure you ask first!). Try something with a wider wooden or plastic frame.

⭐ Your all-time favourite photo of Harry in the whole world (make sure it fits your frame!)

⭐ Lots of One Direction articles and photos of Harry cut out of magazines to decorate the frame with

⭐ Some PVA glue

⭐ A small brush for the glue

⭐ Some glitter to decorate

## What to do:

First lay down some newspaper on a table, so you don't get your mess everywhere (make sure you are wearing an apron or some old clothes too!).

Now you need to arrange your magazine pages. Cut out some sentences from articles about Harry that you like and cut out Harry's name from somewhere, so you can place this at the top of the frame.

Take the back off the frame and take the glass out of the middle, so you're just working with the basic frame. This will stop the glass and the back getting accidentally decorated too.

Now, you need to get gluing! First use the brush to paint a small part of the frame with glue. Then stick your cut out bits to the frame, and paint more glue over them. You need to do this until the whole frame is covered with layers of pictures and words, without any of the original frame showing through.

Be creative and layer things on top of each other and then put Harry's name right at the top of the frame. Glue this down well.

Before the glue dries, take your glitter and sprinkle it all over the frame. Use as much or as little as you like!

Once the glue has dried, you then need to paint over the whole frame with another layer of glue. This will help to hold the glitter in place.

Once the second layer of glue has dried, put the glass back into the frame, add your perfect photo of Harry, and voila! Your very own customised decoupage photo frame! Isn't it dreamy?

# Chapter 5
# LOVE AND STUFF

I ♥ HARRY

**FUN FACT:**
Harry's favourite Christmas film is *It's A Wonderful Life*.

**Cutie Harry has always been the romantic type. Even as far back as being six years old, Harry had a first girlfriend called Phoebe – who he bought a teddy bear for!**

Although he had a few other girlfriends when he was a bit younger, he started going out with his first proper girlfriend at the age of 12. A couple of years later, his first serious girlfriend was a girl called Abi. None of the relationships ever ended really badly, and Harry is still friends with most of his ex-girlfriends now!

Although Harry has been romantically linked to a couple of girls – including the *X Factor* presenter Caroline Flack – he remains single (so there's still hope, ladies!).

'I'm fine with being single,' says Harry. 'I'm not consciously looking for a girlfriend, but if I meet someone I like it would be great. I do like being with someone and if the right person came along then we'd see what happened.'

**FUN FACT:**
Harry's perfect first date is dinner and a movie. Yes please!

Harry's celebrity crushes are Frankie Sandford and Rihanna.

## What does Harry look for in a girl? ⭐

'I don't have a type,' he says. 'Because with some girls I may not find them attractive immediately, but then I really get to like them because their personality is so attractive. I like someone I can have a conversation with.'

He's also attracted to girls who are cute, with a good sense of humour. He doesn't mind what hair colour they have, but he has said he likes girls with short hair. Harry likes being in relationships, and wants someone he can spoil, and someone he can call, any time of day or night, just to talk to. What a cutie!

## ⭐ Harry's good looks

Good looks definitely run in Harry's family – Harry's friends have always fancied his mum! In fact, once he and the One Direction boys were in a café when Harry's mum walked past, and all the boys wolf-whistled! 'She's a very beautiful woman,' says Harry proudly. 'It was the same at school as well!'

## ☆ Love advice

Although you wouldn't think that Harry or the other One Direction boys need any help when it comes to girls, they do have a brotherly figure they regularly go to for guidance – actor James Corden! 'James gives great advice,' says Harry, who often texts the big man.

## Talking about regrets ☆

Though Harry has been linked to a few lovely ladies, he's yet to have any big and serious relationships. But he doesn't worry about anything he's done in the past. Instead, he chalks everything down to experience: 'I don't usually regret it because if you can't change it, there's no point regretting it.' Wise words for all of us.

**HARRY:** 'I would always look for someone who could get on with my parents. It's important to me that my family like her too.'

# HARRY'S HOROSCOPE

**Harry's birthday is 1st February, which makes him an Aquarius. Want to know the inner secrets of Harry's birthsign? Then read on!**

## Aquarius – the overview

Harry is a typical Aquarian in that he is very independent. He can also be very firm and even stubborn at times. Despite that, Harry is a faithful soul who is very supportive of his friends and family, and super loyal in any relationship.

## Harry and the good side of Aquarius

Harry is a true original. He does whatever he wants to do, and doesn't worry about whether he's following the crowd or not – which usually means people turn to him to see what he's up to.

Typically of his star sign, Harry is generous and sympathetic to the plights of others. He is friendly and always willing to help a friend in need. He is a creative soul, and loves following his heart and his dreams.

## Harry and his dark side. . .

Aquarius can be a troubled sign. Aquarians are often unpredictable and it's often difficult to know how they are feeling. Sometimes they are calm but sometimes they are in chaos – they just follow their emotions without always considering the feelings of other people. Harry needs to be careful he doesn't fall into the traps of the negative behaviours of an Aquarian, as this could lead to arguments and hurting other people. As an Aquarian, Harry's lucky starsign foods are pomegranates and pineapples.

# Are you a good love match to Harry?
## Check the chart below to find out!

| ARIES | TAURUS | GEMINI | CANCER | LEO | VIRGO | LIBRA | SCORPIO | SAGITTARIUS | CAPRICORN | AQUARIUS | PISCES | |
|---|---|---|---|---|---|---|---|---|---|---|---|---|
| ♥ | ♡ | ♥ | ♡ | ♥ | ♡ | ♥ | ♡ | 💔 | ♡ | ♥ | 💔 | **HARRY** |

 **Harry's best starsign matches:**

**LIBRA:** A good match as you are both on the same level.

**AQUARIUS:** This is a great bond – you guys would be happy ever after!

**GEMINI:** You would be best friends first, and romance would follow.

**ARIES:** This would be a fun and lively match, but you might drive each other crazy!

**LEO:** A good match as you are opposites and in many ways opposites often attract.

 **Harry's other love matches**

**Although Harry's best love matches are listed above, you could still have a chance at love with Harry – it just might take a little more work!**

**SCORPIO:** You need to be careful your passionate relationship doesn't change to drive you apart.

**TAURUS:** A pair of stubborn signs that could be too stubborn to make it work out. Practise compromise to stay together.

**VIRGO:** Both signs can be a little cold – remember to be forgiving and generous to each other.

**CANCER:** These two signs could rub each other up the wrong way, or they could have a totally explosive connection!

**CAPRICORN:** Again, two stubborn signs together – remember to compromise!

 **No Way!**

**Other famous Aquarians...**
*Charles Darwin*
*John Travolta*
*James Dean*
*Yoko Ono*

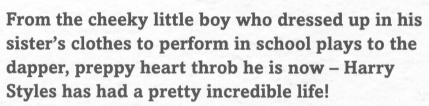

# THE FUTURE!

**From the cheeky little boy who dressed up in his sister's clothes to perform in school plays to the dapper, preppy heart throb he is now – Harry Styles has had a pretty incredible life!**

'Getting into the band through the *X Factor* was such good fortune,' says Harry. 'It was always my dream to perform on stage, and now that's a reality!'

But don't think for a second that Harry hasn't stopped dreaming. From the beginning, he was always ambitious, and now he has different things on his mind. He and the One Direction boys are desperate to break America, and there is even talk of them getting their own TV show out there, like their buddies Big Time Rush, who they opened for on tour.

One thing is for sure though – Harry is going to stay the same, level-headed hottie he was when he first auditioned for the *X Factor*. 'I won't change,' he says. 'I don't want people doing things for me that I could do myself. Sometimes people think they should get me a bottle of water or some lunch, but I'm capable of picking up my own water, so why should they have to do it? My mum would never let me get away with that sort of thing!'

Harry has a lot of hopes for One Direction. The boys are already starting work on their second album, and Harry hopes they can write more songs for it, and play a lot more shows in the meantime.

'We've got a lot of big dreams,' says Harry. 'We like to dream big!' Harry wants to have more number one hits with the band, break the American charts, and travel and have as much fun as possible.

'I don't think that's too much to ask,' he says. And neither do we!

I ♥ HARRY

**FUN FACT:** Harry is the only one in his family with curly hair.

## ACKNOWLEDGEMENTS

Posy Edwards would like to thank Helia Phoenix, Jane Sturrock, Nicola Crossley, Helen Ewing and Richard Carr

Copyright © Orion 2012

First published in hardback in Great Britain in 2012 by
Orion Books an imprint of the Orion Publishing Group Ltd
Orion House, 5 Upper St Martin's Lane, London WC2H 9EA
An Hachette UK Company

1 3 5 7 9 10 8 6 4 2

A CIP catalogue record for this book is available from the British Library.

ISBN: 978 4091 0944 0

Designed by carrdesignstudio.com
Printed and bound in Germany
by Mohn Media

The Orion Publishing Group's policy is to use papers that are natural, renewable and recyclable and made from wood grown in sustainable forests. The logging and manufacturing processes are expected to conform to the environmental regulations of the country of origin.

Every effort has been made to fulfil requirements with regard to reproducing copyright material. The author and publisher will be glad to rectify any omissions at the earliest opportunity.
www.orionbooks.co.uk

## ANSWERS

### WORDSEARCH – p.26

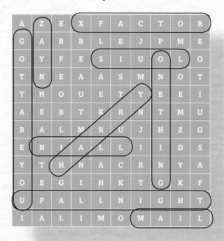

### CROSSWORD – p.27

### HOT HARRY QUIZ – p12

1. Spanish and American accents
2. David Beckham
3. Eyes
4. Tacos
5. Swearing
6. Mango and passion fruit smoothie
7. Carrot
8. Elvis Presley, Freddie Mercury and Michael Jackson
9. Honeycomb
10. Scrambled
11. True
12. False
13. True
14. True
15. His phone, a phone charger and electricity

### ONE DIRECTION QUIZ – p.41

1. Liam
2. Liam
3. Louis
4. Louis
5. Louis
6. Zayn
7. Zayn
8. Niall
9. Niall
10. Harry
11. Harry
12. Harry

## PICTURE CREDITS